TWENTY/TWENTY
PAINTERS/PAINTINGS

TWENTY/TWENTY

PAINTERS / PAINTINGS

LESTER
&ORPEN
DENNYS
PUBLISHERS

CONTEMPORARY CANADIAN ART
SELECTED BY MARCI LIPMAN AND LOUISE LIPMAN

To Peter Gzowski for his inspiration and support

Many people made this book possible. In particular we would like to give special thanks to the artists and their families; Aggregation Gallery: Lynn and David; The Canada Council Art Bank: Lisa Cohen and Chris Youngs; Canadian Eskimo Arts Council; The Innuit Gallery of Eskimo Art: Ruby and Razie; Isaacs Gallery: Av Isaacs; London Regional Art Gallery: Barry Fair; Mira Godard Gallery; The National Gallery of Canada: Susan Campbell and Peter Smith; Sanavik Eskimo Cooperative; Triple K Co-operative; and also to Karyn Allen, Mary Geatros, Pam and Gordon Gibson, Mel Hurtig, Faye Loeb, Aaron Milrad and Yetty Agnew, and David Silcox. Finally, we want to thank our friends and colleagues who encouraged us and helped us.

Printed by Herzig Somerville Limited

Colour separations by Herzig Somerville Limited

Typesetting by Cooper & Beatty Limited

Bound by Holmes Bindery Services Limited

Design by Paul Hodgson for Fifty Fingers

Production by Verbatim

Photographs by Robert Barnett, p. 21; John Evans, p. 11; Fischer Fine Art Ltd., p. 17; Tom Moore, p. 7, 9, 19, 23, 27, 29, 31, 37, 39, 41, 45; Rick Morgan, p. 43; The National Gallery of Canada, p. 13, 15, 25, 33; André Nufer for Design Associates, p. 35

Canadian Cataloguing in Publication Data

Main entry under title:
TWENTY/TWENTY

ISBN 0-919630-10-3

1. Painting, Canadian. 2. Painting, Modern-20th century–Canada. I. Lipman, Marci, 1948–
II. Lipman, Louise, 1953–

ND245.T84   759.11   C79-094567-3

Printed and bound in Canada

TWENTY/TWENTY is an unusual book – the first of its kind in Canada. Twenty paintings by twenty painters – large-size, fine-art reproductions that can be enjoyed as a book or framed separately. As a book TWENTY/TWENTY will reveal something of the excitement of contemporary Canadian art – as a collection of individual paintings it is a gallery in itself.

Since 1974 we have been selling fine-art reproductions and posters from Europe and the United States in our graphics stores, aware all the time of a growing demand for reproductions of works by Canadian artists. But it was impossible to meet the demand because so few reproductions were available – even though American and European artists have had their works reproduced and distributed internationally for years now. These fine-art reproductions have made one-of-a-kind paintings readily available to everyone; their cost is a fraction of that of an original painting, and while the originals are usually out of reach in private collections or local galleries, reproductions can be purchased everywhere. The wide-scale distribution of American and European reproductions has given the artists a degree of public recognition and public support that otherwise would not exist.

So this year, to mark the fifth anniversary of our Toronto store, we published two posters of paintings by Canadian artists Bruce St. Clair and John Lander. The response was overwhelming. It emphasized the need for reproductions of Canadian works. It also showed that it would take more than the publication of one or two posters to satisfy that need.

TWENTY/TWENTY is our answer – a book of twenty paintings by twenty painters. And what encouraged us most along the way was the enthusiasm of the artists themselves for the project. They liked the idea of having their work made accessible to the public, and those who could provided us with a comment on the painting we chose. This is really their book.

Our greatest difficulty was limiting ourselves to twenty artists, and to only one painting from each artist. There are many artists we would like to have included and had to leave out – art in Canada is so rich and multi-faceted that with twenty paintings we have just scratched the surface. But TWENTY/TWENTY is a beginning. We intend it to be the first of several books in this format.

In making our selection we have tried to provide an overview of contemporary Canadian art. We have selected artists from every region of the country, and have looked for a cross-section of techniques, styles and themes (including, for example, high realism, still life, abstract, landscape and native art). Great care was taken in the printing to be faithful to the originals. The paintings are representative of the artists' styles and, in many cases, are their most recent work. None has ever before been reproduced in this format, and a number are brand new – the paint on Greg Curnoe's "Mariposa T.T." was still wet when we put the book together; Alex Colville had just completed "Main Street"; and we found Louis deNiverville's "In Hope of Spring" at a personal preview of his new work. Some of the artists are well known in Canada and abroad; others are just beginning to establish a reputation.

From the outset we hoped to create a book that would suggest the range and mood of art in this country, and in a way that would allow each individual work to stand on its own. The intention and design of TWENTY/TWENTY is that each painting can be taken out and framed for a personal collection – but seen together the twenty individual paintings reflect in spirit and imagination what is happening in Canadian art today.

Marci Lipman was born in Toronto and studied Fine Arts at York University. She is a leading art consultant, and the owner of Marci Lipman Graphics – Canada's major fine-arts poster house with stores in Toronto and Calgary. Louise Lipman studied at Bard College and the University of British Columbia and is a design consultant. She has worked with her sister Marci for the past five years.

Bruce St. Clair
"Three Chairs"
Oil on panel, 16″ x 13½″, 1978
Crown Life Collection of Canadian Art

"'Three Chairs' is full of remembering backwards and
forwards–time passing through its three tenses. It starts
now, the initial impression. Light, and things standing in the
way of light. Space and confinement; atmosphere and
porch paint; three chairs the colour of traffic lights. And a
few fallen leaves in memory of past summers. But just
beyond there are barriers and the far shore."

Anguhadlug / Akuliaq
"Caribou Grazing"
Silkscreen, edition of 60, 22" × 30", July 1979
Reproduced with permission of the Sanavik Eskimo Cooperative,
Baker Lake, North West Territories;
courtesy of The Innuit Gallery of Eskimo Art, Toronto

Gordon Smith
"Untitled"
Acrylic on paper, 24¼" x 30¼", June 1975
Collection: The Canada Council Art Bank, Ottawa

"I have lived and worked by the ocean most of my life–each
day throughout the year I look out over the Straits of
Georgia–I see the sea and the sky with all their changing
moods. I do not set out to reproduce what I see but to
recreate how I feel about the subject, and in the process of
painting subject and technique become inseparable–for me
painting in this way tends toward a complete interlocking of
image and paint–so that the image is paint and vice versa."

David Milne
"White Poppies"
Watercolour, 14⅝" x 21⅜", 1946
Collection: The National Gallery of Canada, Ottawa

Jack Bush
"Tall Spread"
Acrylic polymer on canvas, 107" x 50¼", 1966
Collection: The National Gallery of Canada, Ottawa

Alex Colville
"Main Street"
Acrylic polymer emulsion, 61 cm x 86.2 cm, 1979
Courtesy of Fischer Fine Art Ltd., London, England

"I have thought over the last quarter-century of doing
something with a World War I memorial statue. Finally last
autumn, on armistice day, I began to have an idea of how I
could handle this theme by using a statue as an apparent
backdrop for a contemporary shopping trip, with two
women bringing groceries to a contemporary car. I think of
World War I as the major watershed in modern
history—our lives have been shaped by it. So the painting
might be said to be about living in the present while being
aware of the past; it is also about women and men."

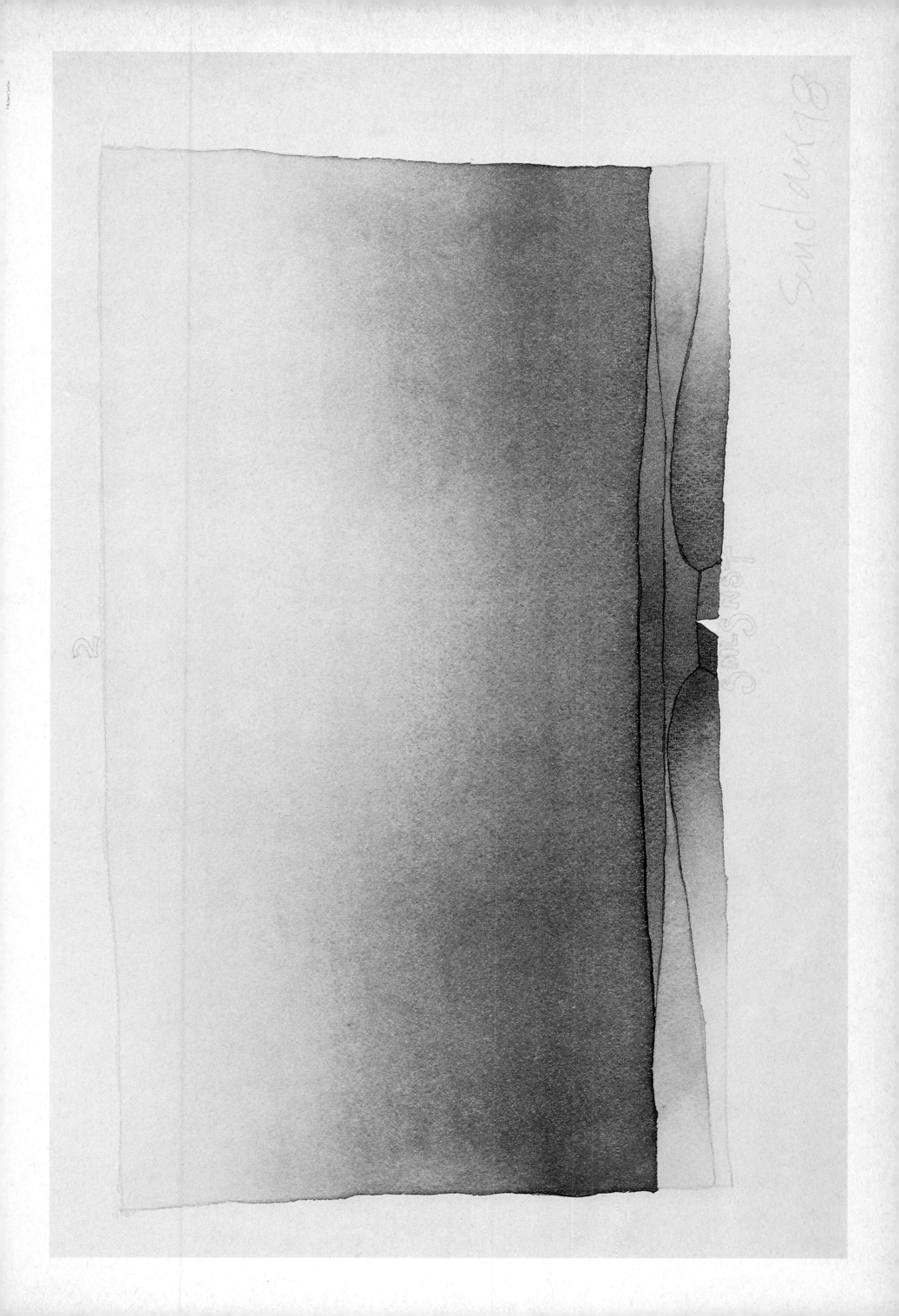

Robert Sinclair
"Small Sunset"
Watercolour on arches paper, 7½" x 11", 1978
Private collection

"I believe art is meant to be enjoyed. It is a mind's playing
become tangible."

William Kurelek
"Eve be soon"
Mixed media, 4′ x 4′, 1970
Private collection

Mary Pratt
"Fish on a Red Plate"
Oil on panel, 11" x 14", 1974
Courtesy of Aggregation Gallery, Toronto

"On May 24th my children caught thirty-two trout. This
was not something that happened every day. Even though
we live only a few yards from a trout river, the children
have never particularly enjoyed fishing (the rule that they
had to clean what they caught may have been something of
a deterrent!). It was the most classic painting of the series,
the most colourful, and the simplest. Probably that is why I
now feel that it is one of the most successful images to
emerge from that May 24th holiday."

Jean Paul Lemieux
"La Visite"
Oil on canvas, 67" x 42", year uncertain
Collection: The National Gallery of Canada, Ottawa

"It's for the onlooker to try and find something in my
painting. I can't. Time will tell I suppose."

60/60   Loonie Nocturnal Call   Douglas Tokagumie Ian ©

Goyce Kakagemic
"Loon's Nocturnal Call"
Serigraph on arches paper, 22" x 30", 1977
Courtesy of the Triple K Co-operative, Red Lake, Ontario,
and Aggregation Gallery, Toronto

"My work reflects the legends, heritage and experience of
my people, the Cree of Northern Ontario. The loon's call
at sunset is still a familiar occurrence across the lakes of this
part of the country."

Dorothy Knowles
"Summer Day"
Oil on canvas, 30″ x 36″, 1969
Collection: Mary Geatros

John Lander
"Fifth Anniversary"
Airbrush, watercolour and acrylic paint on paper, 35½″ × 25″, 1979
Collection: Marci Lipman

"'Fifth Anniversary' was the first in a series of drawings
entitled 'Chinaman's Bouquet.' The line used in the series
was to be strong enough to exist alone and only give
inference to area. In 'Fifth Anniversary' the line did not
satisfy this requirement (disqualifying the work from
the series) but the drawing did make a satisfactory plan for
a composition of colour and area. Dealing with area
rather than line, recognizing line as a boundary, area
became delineated by colour and modulation. Line
disappeared. The result is a composition of modulated
colour areas describing a floral arrangement."

James Spencer
"Wave # 4"
Acrylic on canvas, 108″ x 132″, 1972-3
Collection: The National Gallery of Canada, Ottawa

"I am interested in painting 'natural' things–water,
mountains, animals, people, etc.–these images, their
motion and reflection of light."

© Greg Curnoe

Greg Curnoe
"Mariposa T.T."
Watercolour in life-size, 110.5 cm x 179.7 cm, December 29, 1978–February 28, 1979
Courtesy of the artist

"'Mariposa T.T.' is the second watercolour I have made of
this subject. The bicycle is a custom-built 5-speed time-trial
racing machine. This version was painted while I was
working on an edition of serigraphs of the same bicycle on
plexiglass at 'Editions Canada'. The equipment is
constantly changing on this machine as lighter parts are
added. It now weighs under 18 lbs. Ironically, as the bike
gets lighter my times seem to get slower (I rode a
1.03.04 25-mile time trial on this bike in 1977)."

Joseph Devellano
"Free Ride"
Egg tempera on panel, 24″ × 36″, 1977-8
Private collection

"This is a critical observation made while walking in a place
I remembered as fun and exciting. Other things
overshadowed the memories and arrested a fantasy
with reality."

Charlie Pachter
"Streetcar Headdress"
Collaged silkscreen, 24" x 30", 1976
Courtesy of the artist

"I have had an on-going love affair with streetcars as long as
I can remember. Once, at the age of seven or so, I sent
box tops to a cereal company offering a genuine cardboard
streetcar to all loyal Shreddie munchers. I anxiously awaited
its arrival. The streetcar never came. So, years later,
I made my own. 'Streetcar Headdress' is one version from
a series of collaged silkscreens."

Louis deNiverville
"In Hope of Spring"
Acrylic and airbrush on canvas, 36″ × 42″, 1979
Collection: John and Susan Potts

"This still life was conceived in the dead of winter from a
seed catalogue: note the hothouse colours. The rabbit was
a latecomer and to my mind gave this image its
raison d'être."

Christopher Pratt
"Shop on an Island"
Oil on board, 81.3 cm x 91.4 cm, 1969
Gift of Mr J. H. Moore through the Ontario Heritage Foundation
to the London Regional Art Gallery, London, Ontario

"If I couldn't be a painter, I wouldn't know what to do: as a
painter, I don't know any other way to do it."

20/20

Rita Letendre
"Unga"
Acrylic on canvas, 78" x 64", 1978
Courtesy of the artist

"Art is an expression of what a person feels about the
whole world and the position of that person in the world. It
is a type of self-commentary. My painting is non-figurative,
abstract, maybe it's lyrical—all this terminology is
not important; *what is important is the actual painting*."

BIOGRAPHIES

BRUCE ST. CLAIR was born in 1945 in Galt, Ontario. After attending the Ontario College of Art in Toronto he travelled widely around Ontario, painting and studying on his own. He settled in the Lake Nipissing area of Northern Ontario in 1969.

LUKE ANGUHADLUG was born in 1894. He has lived in camps—fishing and hunting—and has worked at The Print Shop in Baker Lake, North West Territories, since it started in 1967.

T. AKULIAQ is a very young man, about 24 years old. He spends half the year on the land, trying to become a good hunter. He has just recently begun to work at The Print Shop in Baker Lake.

GORDON SMITH, born in 1919 in Hove, England, came to Canada in 1934 and settled in Winnipeg. He studied at the Winnipeg School of Art under LeMoine FitzGerald. After serving in the Canadian army he moved to Vancouver, teaching graphics and commercial design at the Vancouver School and eventually joining the Faculty of Education at the University of British Columbia. In the interim he also studied at Harvard University and under Elmer Bischoff at the California School of Fine Arts.

DAVID MILNE was born in 1882 in Paisley, Ontario, and in 1904 moved to New York. He studied at night at the Art Students League and worked in the day as a commercial artist. He lived and worked in New York and the Lower Berkshires until the outbreak of war when he enlisted in the Canadian army. In 1919 he was made an official war artist in England. After the war Milne travelled between the Berkshires and Ottawa. He finally settled in Baptiste Lake, Ontario, after spending several years in small towns in Ontario and the Canadian bush. He died in 1953.

JACK BUSH was born in Toronto in 1909 and died there in 1977. Educated at the Royal Canadian Academy in Montreal, and at the Ontario College of Art, he studied at night and worked as a commercial artist during the day. In 1952 he made the first of a series of trips to New York to study the originals of paintings that he had only seen reproduced in magazines. These trips, together with his association with Clement Greenberg—whom he met in 1957 when Greenberg was invited to Toronto by the Group of Eleven, of which Jack Bush was a member—were very influential. In 1968 he retired from advertising work to concentrate fully on his painting for which he has won international acclaim.

ALEX COLVILLE was born in Toronto in 1920, and moved to Amherst, Nova Scotia at the age of nine. He studied Fine Arts under Stanley Royle at Mount Allison University, New Brunswick. From 1944-46 he was an official war artist in the Mediterranean and Northern Europe, returning to teach at Mount Allison until 1963. He now paints full time and lives in Wolfville, Nova Scotia.

ROBERT SINCLAIR was born in Saltcoats, Saskatchewan, in 1939. He studied at the University of Manitoba School of Art and at the University of Iowa Department of Anthropology and History, and has since taught at the University of Alberta in the Department of Art and Design. He was Artist-in-Residence at the University of Iowa and the Banff School of Fine Arts, and now lives in the country near Edmonton.

WILLIAM KURELEK was born in 1927 in Whitford, Alberta. He graduated from the University of Manitoba in 1949 but he was mainly a self-taught painter. He studied part time at the Ontario College of Art under Frederick Hagan, and at the Institute Allende in Mexico, under Pinto and Baldwin. He lived in England from 1952-59, and travelled through Jordan and Israel before returning to Toronto where he had his first show at the Isaacs Gallery in the early 60's. He died in Toronto in November 1977.

MARY PRATT, born in 1935 in Fredericton, New Brunswick, studied at the University of New Brunswick Summer School under Fritz Banter and G. Pinsky, and at Mount Allison School of Fine Arts. As the mother of four children, she had little time to devote to her painting until 1965. She now lives and works in St. Mary's Bay, Newfoundland.

JEAN PAUL LEMIEUX was born in Quebec City in 1904. He studied with the Brothers of the Christian Schools in California, returning to Montreal in 1917 to Loyola College. He subsequently attended the Ecole des Beaux Arts, Quebec, until 1934—including a year of study in Paris in 1929. From 1937 to 1965 he taught at the Ecole des Beaux Arts. Today he lives and paints in Quebec City and Isles aux Coudres, Quebec.

GOYCE KAKAGEMIC was born on the Sandy Lake Reserve, Ontario, in 1948. He is a self-taught artist. He now lives in Red Lake, Ontario.

DOROTHY KNOWLES was born in Unity, Saskatchewan, in 1927. After attending the University of Saskatchewan she studied at the Goldsmith School of Art in London, England, and then under such teachers as Clement Greenberg, Will Barnet and Jules Olitsky at the Emma Lake Summer School, Saskatchewan. She lives in Saskatoon with her husband William Perehudoff.

JOHN LANDER was born in Oshawa, Ontario, in 1951. He studied at the Banff School of Fine Arts, and then at York University in Toronto. He lives in Toronto.

JAMES SPENCER, born in 1940, Wolfville, Nova Scotia, attended Acadia University and the Ontario College of Art. He has taught art at Central Technical School, Toronto; Mohawk College, Hamilton; Dundas Valley School of Art; McMaster University, Hamilton, and the Banff School of Fine Arts. He lives in Toronto.

GREG CURNOE lives in London, Ontario, where he was born in 1936. After studying under Herb Ariss at H. B. Beal Technical School, he spent a summer at the Doon School of Fine Art in Kitchener, and then attended the Ontario College of Art in Toronto. He returned to London to help found the Region Magazine and the Nihilist party, was involved in the Neo-Dada Exhibition at the Isaacs Gallery, and arranged the Celebration—a happening at the London Arts Museum. He represented Canada at the São Paulo Bienal in Brazil.

JOSEPH DEVELLANO lives in Hamilton, Ontario, where he was born in 1945. He studied at the Ontario College of Art from 1964-67.

CHARLIE PACHTER lives in Toronto, where he was born in 1942. He studied at the Sorbonne, the University of Toronto and the Cranbrooke Academy of Art, and has been involved in art consulting, set design, graphic design and illustrating. He was an instructor at the West Baffin Eskimo Co-operative, Cape Dorset, and assistant professor at the University of Calgary Department of Art.

LOUIS deNIVERVILLE, born in 1925 in Andover, England, came to Canada in 1934 and settled in Montreal. He is a self-taught painter. He has also illustrated children's books and has worked in the theatre as a designer. He spent some time in Ottawa before moving to Toronto where he now lives.

CHRISTOPHER PRATT was born in St. John's, Newfoundland, in 1935. His grandfather encouraged him to paint from a very young age, although before attending the Glasgow School of Fine Arts in 1957 he briefly studied both engineering at Memorial University, St. Johns, and medicine at Mount Allison University, New Brunswick. In 1959 he returned again to Mount Allison, studying under Alex Colville, Lawren Harris and Edward Pulford. He himself taught art at Memorial for two years, before moving in 1963 to St. Mary's Bay, Newfoundland, where he lives with his wife Mary Pratt.

RITA LETENDRE was born in 1929 in Drummondville, Quebec. She studied at the Ecole des Beaux Arts in Montreal before becoming a student of Paul-Emile Borduas. She has since lived in Europe, California, and in New York; she moved to Toronto in 1969.